EXPLORE THE FANTASTIC WORLD OF

BIRDS

PICTURE ENCYCLOPEDIA

Wonder House

HARPY EAGLE

The Harpy Eagle is a majestic raptor with striking plumage, characterized by its dark gray body, white underparts and a distinctive black crest of feathers on its head. This powerful bird weighs about 13–22lb (6–10kg), making it one of the largest eagles. It preys on medium-sized mammals and birds, such as Monkeys and Sloths. It is native to the tropical rainforests of Central and South America. The Harpy Eagle's formidable claws, called talons, and strong beak make it a top predator in its forested habitat. Belonging to the family ***Accipitridae***, its scientific name is ***Harpia harpyja***.

Of all Eagles, Harpy has the largest talons. These are as large as Grizzly Bear claws.

BALD EAGLE

The Bald Eagle is a majestic bird of prey, known for its striking appearance. With a mass ranging from 6.6–13.9lb (3–6.3kg), it boasts a formidable presence. Its plumage features a dark brown body with a distinctive white head and tail, while its beak and claws are bright yellow. The Bald Eagle primarily feeds on fish, but also hunts small mammals and birds. It is a symbol of strength and freedom. It is a member of the family ***Accipitridae***. The scientific name of the Bald Eagle is ***Haliaeetus leucocephalus***.

DID YOU KNOW?

Bald Eagles have up to 8ft (2.4m) wingspan, which is as wide as a car!

BLACK VULTURE

The Black Vulture is a large bird with dark, sooty-black plumage, a bare, wrinkled black head and short, square tail. Measuring about 24in (61cm) in length, this scavenger primarily feeds on carrion but occasionally consumes small animals and eggs. Black Vultures inhabit open areas, including shrublands, and deserts, often near human settlements. They are highly social birds, often seen soaring in flocks, relying on their keen eyesight to locate food. It belongs to the family ***Cathartidae*** and its scientific name is ***Coragyps atratus***.

PEREGRINE FALCON

The Peregrine Falcon is a powerful bird of prey known for its speed and agility. It has a compact, muscular body and long, pointed wings, it weighs about 21–53oz (600–1,500g). Its wingspan can reach to a length of 3.5ft (1m). This falcon feeds mainly on birds and inhabits diverse environments, from mountains to coastlines. It belongs to the family ***Falconidae*** and its scientific name is ***Falco peregrinus***.

DID YOU KNOW?

The Peregrine Falcon is the fastest bird in the world, reaching speeds of over 200mph (321.8kph) while diving!

DID YOU KNOW?

They are named for their crest feathers, which look like a secretary's quill pen stuck behind their head!

SECRETARY BIRD

The Secretary Bird is a tall, slender bird of prey known for its long legs and distinctive crest of black feathers. Weighing around 7.3–9.5lb (3.3–4.3kg), the Secretary Bird feeds primarily on Snakes, insects and small mammals. Found in sub-Saharan Africa's savannas and grasslands, it stalks prey on foot. It belongs to the family ***Sagittariidae*** and its scientific name is ***Sagittarius serpentarius***.

EURASIAN EAGLE OWL

The Eurasian Eagle Owl is one of the world's largest owls, with a body length of about 2.5ft (76cm) and a weight ranging from 3.3–9.3lb (1.5–4.2kg). This owl has a striking appearance with bright orange eyes, prominent ear tufts and dense, mottled brown feathers. Its diet includes small mammals, birds and even reptiles, which it hunts from perches at night. Found across Europe and Asia, it inhabits rocky cliffs and woodlands. This owl is well-adapted to diverse habitats and climates. Belonging to the family ***Strigidae***, its scientific name is ***Bubo bubo***.

DID YOU KNOW?

The Eurasian Eagle Owl's wingspan of 6.5ft (2m).

HOUSE SPARROW

The House Sparrow is a small, plump bird with a short tail and a stout beak. Males typically have a gray crown, black bib and chestnut-colored nape, while females are more uniformly brown with streaked backs and pale underparts. Sparrows weigh around 0.8–1.4oz (24–40g). Their diet consists mainly of seeds, grains and small insects. These adaptable birds are commonly found in urban and suburban areas, often near human habitation. They thrive in a wide range of habitats globally. Belonging to the family ***Passeridae***, their scientific name is ***Passer domesticus***.

DID YOU KNOW?

Their song is a melody of chirp notes, often heard in residential and agricultural areas.

STARLING

The Starling is a medium-sized bird with iridescent black feathers that shimmer in shades of green and purple, especially during the breeding season. Weighing around 2.6–3.2oz (75–90g). Starlings primarily feed on insects, fruits and seeds. They inhabit open fields, urban areas and woodlands across Europe, Asia and North America. Starlings are known for their incredible murmurations, creating mesmerizing aerial displays. Belonging to the family ***Sturnidae***, their scientific name is ***Sturnus vulgaris***.

DID YOU KNOW?

Starlings can mimic the sound of other birds, and even mechanical noises.

HOUSE FINCH

The House Finch is a small bird. Male Finches showcase bright red plumage on their heads, throats and chests, while females have brown streaks. They typically weigh from 0.6–0.9oz (17–27g). They primarily eat seeds, fruits and buds. House Finches are commonly found in urban areas, gardens and forests across North America. Belonging to the family ***Fringillidae***, their scientific name is ***Haemorhous mexicanus***.

DID YOU KNOW?

They sometimes build their nests in unusual places, like on hanging plants or porch lights!

AMERICAN ROBIN

The American Robin is a small, agile bird with a mass of about 2.7–3oz (77–85g). It primarily feeds on insects, worms and berries. This Robin inhabits a variety of environments, including forests, gardens and grasslands throughout North America. Its striking appearance features a bright orange-red breast, grey-brown back and a white belly, making it a recognizable and cheerful presence in its habitat. Its song in the morning sounds like "cheerily, cheer up, cheer up, cheerily..." Belonging to the family ***Turdidae***, the scientific name for the American Robin is ***Turdus migratorius***.

DID YOU KNOW?

Baby Robins grow fast and leave the nest in just 2 weeks!

DID YOU KNOW?

They have been named as the official bird of at least 7 states of the Americas.

NORTHERN CARDINAL

The Northern Cardinal is a striking bird with vibrant red plumage that covers its body, accented by a black mask around its face and a crest on its head. A Female Northern Cardinal is more subdued, with brownish tones and hints of red. This bird weighs around 1.6oz (45g). It primarily feeds on seeds, fruits and insects. It is part of the ***Cardinalidae*** family. The scientific name of the Northern Cardinal is ***Cardinalis cardinalis***.

BLUE JAY

The Blue Jay is a striking bird with vibrant blue feathers on its back, wings and tail, complemented by white underparts and a black collar around its neck. They have a white face with a bold black "mask" and blue crest on their head. Weighing around 2.5–3.5oz (70–100g) and reaching about 9.8–11.8in (25–30cm) in length, Blue Jays are omnivores, eating insects, nuts and seeds. Native to North America, Blue Jays are often found in forests, parks and suburban areas. They are known for their loud calls and intelligence. Belonging to the family ***Corvidae*** and the order ***Passeriformes***, their scientific name is ***Cyanocitta cristata***.

DID YOU KNOW?

Blue Jays can make a variety of sounds for different purposes.

REDSTART

The Redstart is a small, slender bird known for its vibrant coloring and distinctive tail movements. Males are particularly striking, with bright orange-red underparts, a slate-gray head and a black face mask, while females look more subdued in brown and gray but share the same red-orange tail. Weighing around 0.4–0.7oz (11–20g) and about 5.5in (14cm) in length, Redstarts feed primarily on insects, berries and small invertebrates. Their preferred habitats include woodlands, open forests and gardens across Europe and Asia. They migrate seasonally, flying to warmer regions during winters. They belong to the family ***Muscicapidae*** and their scientific name is ***Phoenicurus phoenicurus***.

DID YOU KNOW?

Redstarts prefer spending most of their time on trees rather than on the ground.

OLIVE-BACKED TAILORBIRD

The Olive-Backed Tailorbird is a small, vibrant bird with an olive-green back and a distinct, bright yellow underbelly. It measures about 4.3in (11cm) long and feeds mainly on insects and larvae. It inhabits dense tropical and subtropical forests, as well as shrublands in Southeast Asia. Its compact size and colorful plumage makes it a striking presence in its habitat. It belongs to the family ***Cisticolidae*** and its scientific name is ***Orthotomus sepium***.

DID YOU KNOW?

The Olive-backed Tailorbird stitches leaves together to make a cozy nest, almost like sewing clothes!

EUROPEAN CRESTED TIT

The European Crested Tit is a small, distinctive bird with a prominent crest of feathers on its head, a white face and a brownish-grey body. With a length of 4.3–4.7in (11–12cm), it weighs about 0.3–0.4oz (8.5–11g). This bird primarily feeds on insects, seeds and nuts. Its natural habitat includes coniferous forests across Europe, particularly in mountainous and wooded areas. The bird belongs to the family ***Paridae*** and its scientific name is ***Lophophanes cristatus***.

DID YOU KNOW?

It has a special "pocket" in its throat to store extra food for later.

OLIVE-BACKED SUNBIRD

The Olive-Backed Sunbird is a small, colorful bird with a vibrant greenish-yellow belly and a contrasting olive-brown back. A Male Sunbird has a striking iridescent blue throat and chest. Measuring about 4.7in (12cm) long, this sunbird feeds primarily on nectar from flowers, supplemented by insects. It is commonly found in tropical and subtropical forests, gardens and urban areas across China, Southeast Asia, including Malaysia, Thailand and the Philippines. It belongs to the family ***Nectariniidae*** and its scientific name is ***Cinnyris jugularis***.

DID YOU KNOW?

The Female Olive-Backed Sunbird lays 1–2 greenish-blue eggs at a time.

CANARY

The Canary is a small, brightly colored bird, known for its vibrant yellow plumage, though it can also be found in shades of green and orange. Measuring about 5.5in (14cm), Canaries primarily feed on seeds, fruits and vegetables. These birds are native to the Canary Islands, Azores and Madeira, but have been widely domesticated and kept as pets worldwide. In the wild, they inhabit subtropical forests, shrublands and gardens. As caged birds, they can survive for 10–15 years. Belonging to the family ***Fringillidae***, their scientific name is ***Serinus canaria***.

DID YOU KNOW?

Canaries were once used in coal mines to warn miners of dangerous gases.

HUMMINGBIRD

The Hummingbird is a vibrant, tiny bird with a maximum length reaching only 7.8in (20cm), known for its iridescent plumage that can range from brilliant greens to dazzling reds and blues. Typically weighing around 0.07–0.7oz (2–20g), these birds feed primarily on flower nectar, supplemented with small insects and Spiders for protein. They inhabit a variety of environments from tropical rainforests to temperate gardens. Belonging to the family ***Trochilidae***, their scientific name depends upon the species.

DID YOU KNOW?

Hummingbirds are the only birds that can fly backwards!

ZITTING CISTICOLA

The Zitting Cisticola is a small, brownish bird with streaked upperparts and a lighter, pale underside. Its tail is short, often cocked and displays black and white tips. It measures about 4.3in (11cm) and its diet mainly consists of insects. The bird thrives in grasslands, wetlands and open fields across Africa, southern Europe and Asia. It's well known for its distinctive "zitting" call during flight. Belonging to the family ***Cisticolidae***, its scientific name is ***Cisticola juncidis***.

DID YOU KNOW?

It builds its nest in tall grass, like a little house in a meadow.

DID YOU KNOW?

Eastern Meadowlarks build their nests on the ground for safety.

EASTERN MEADOWLARK

The Eastern Meadowlark is a medium-sized songbird with bright yellow underparts and a distinctive black "V" shape on its chest. Its upperparts are streaked with brown, black and white, providing excellent camouflage in grasslands. Weighing from 2.8–5.3oz (80–150g), this bird feeds on insects and seeds. It thrives in open fields and meadows across eastern North America. Belonging to the family ***Icteridae*** and the order ***Passeriformes***, its scientific name is ***Sturnella magna***.

CHICKADEE

The Chickadee is a small, endearing bird with distinctive coloring. Their body features soft gray wings with a creamy white underside, a striking black cap and a matching black bib, making them easily recognizable. Weighing about 0.3–0.5oz (8.5–14g), Chickadees primarily feed on insects, seeds and berries. They inhabit forests, woodlands and suburban areas across North America. Chickadees are agile and quick, known for their curious and lively nature as they flit through branches searching for food. They belong to the family ***Paridae***. Of the 13 species, the scientific name of the Black-Capped Chickadee is ***Poecile atricapillus***.

MAGPIE

The Magpie is a striking bird with black and white plumage, a long tail and iridescent blue-green wings. These birds measure less than 19in (48cm) in length. Magpies are omnivores, feeding on insects, small mammals, fruits and seeds. They are commonly found in open woodlands, farmlands and urban areas across Europe, Asia and North America. Their adaptability allows them to thrive in various habitats. Magpies belong to the family ***Corvidae***. The scientific name of one of the common species, the Eurasian Magpie is ***Pica pica***.

DID YOU KNOW?

Magpies are songbirds that produce harsh and noisy calls.

MOUNTAIN BLUEBIRD

The Mountain Bluebird is a striking bird with vibrant sky-blue plumage in males and a more subdued grayish-blue in females. Weighing around 0.8–1.1oz (24–31g), this bird primarily feeds on insects and berries, making it an adept forager in open country. The Mountain Bluebird is found in habitats ranging from grasslands to alpine regions across western North America. It belongs to the family ***Turdidae***. The scientific name for the Mountain Bluebird is ***Sialia currucoides***.

DID YOU KNOW?

During winter, they migrate from their mountain homes to low-elevated areas to stay cozy.

COMMON MYNA

The Common Myna is a medium-sized bird known for its dark brown body, black head and bright yellow eye patches, beak and legs. Weighing around 4.2–4.9oz (120–140g), Mynas are omnivorous, feeding on fruits, insects and small animals. They are highly adaptable and can be found in a variety of habitats, including urban areas, farmlands and forests across Asia. They belong to the family ***Sturnidae*** and the order ***Passeriformes***, and their scientific name is ***Acridotheres tristis***.

DID YOU KNOW?

If kept as a pet, it imitates human speech better than a parrot.

HOOPOE

The Hoopoe is a striking bird known for its unique crest, which it fans out when excited. Its plumage is a mix of cinnamon-orange with black and white striped wings and tail. The beak is long and slender, ideal for probing the ground for insects and larvae, its primary food. Weighing around 1.6–3.1oz (45–89g), it inhabits open landscapes like savannas, grasslands and orchards across Europe, Asia and Africa. The Hoopoe belongs to the family ***Upupidae*** and its scientific name is ***Upupa epops***.

DID YOU KNOW?

Hoopoe is the national bird of Israel.

DID YOU KNOW?

European Bee-Eaters love to eat Bees but remove the stingers first!

EUROPEAN BEE-EATER

The European Bee-Eater is a vibrantly colored bird with a striking mix of green, blue, yellow and brown plumage. Its slender body, ranging from 9.8–11.4in (25–29cm) in length, and pointed wings make it an agile flyer. This bird primarily feeds on bees and other flying insects. It inhabits open landscapes, such as savannas and farmlands, across Europe, North Africa and parts of Asia. Belonging to the family ***Meropidae***, its scientific name is ***Merops apiaster***.

WOODCHAT SHRIKE

The Woodchat Shrike is a small passerine bird, weighing around 1–1.4oz (30–40g) and measuring about 6.7–7.8in (17–20cm) in length. Its plumage is a striking contrast of black, white and reddish-brown on the head. The wings and back are black, while underparts are white. The Woodchat Shrike feeds on insects, small mammals and birds. It inhabits open woodlands and scrub areas across Europe and North Africa. Classified family ***Laniidae***, the scientific name for the Woodchat Shrike is ***Lanius senator***.

DID YOU KNOW?

They often impale their food on thorns to save it for later!

VERMILION FLYCATCHER

The Vermilion Flycatcher is a striking bird, known for its vibrant red plumage in males, contrasted with dark brown wings and tail. Whereas, a Female Vermilion Flycatcher is less vivid, featuring pale underparts and brownish upperparts. Weighing around 0.4–0.5oz (11–14g), this bird primarily feeds on insects, catching them mid-flight. Found in open woodland, scrublands and near water bodies, it inhabits regions across the Americas. It belongs to the family ***Tyrannidae***, and its scientific name is ***Pyrocephalus rubinus***.

DID YOU KNOW?

They're great acrobats, catching bugs midair while sitting on high fences.

INDIGO BUNTING

The Indigo Bunting is a small, striking bird known for its brilliant blue plumage in males, while females are brown with subtle streaks. It weighs around 0.4–0.6oz (11–17g). It primarily feeds on seeds, insects and berries. This bird thrives in habitats like open woodlands, brushy areas and fields in eastern America. The Indigo Bunting migrates seasonally, spending winters in Central America and the Caribbean. Belonging to the family ***Cardinalidae***, their scientific name is ***Passerina yanea***.

DID YOU KNOW?

Indigo Buntings migrate at night to long distances with stars to guide them.

GALÁPAGOS FINCH

The Galápagos Finch, also known as Darwin's Finch, weighs about 0.3–1.3oz (8.5–38g), has a variety of beak shapes and sizes, adapted to different food sources like seeds, insects and nectar. These birds are key examples of adaptive radiation. Their plumage is typically dull brown or black, blending with their volcanic island habitat. Belonging to the family ***Emberizidae***, these Finches are native to the Galápagos Islands and Cocos Island, including several species within the genera ***Geospiza***, ***Certhidea*** and ***Camarhynchus***.

DID YOU KNOW?

The shape of the beak of Galápagos Finch can differ depending on what it eats!

SWALLOW

The Swallow is a small, agile bird with glossy blue-black upperparts, a reddish-brown throat and a distinctive forked tail. Swallows primarily feed on flying insects, catching them midair with remarkable speed. They inhabit open areas such as fields, meadows, are found near bodies of water and often seen building nests in barns or under bridges. With around 40 species worldwide, they belong to the family ***Hirundinidae***. The scientific name of the Common Swallow is ***Hirundo rustica***.

DID YOU KNOW?

Swallows build their nests out of mud, and often attach them to buildings or cliff faces.

WHITE-RUMPED SHAMA

The White-Rumped Shama is a small, striking bird with glossy black plumage, a white rump and a rich chestnut belly. The Male Shama is particularly vibrant, measuring about 8.3–9.8in (21–25cm). This bird primarily feeds on insects and small invertebrates. It thrives in dense forests and shrublands across South and Southeast Asia. It is known for its melodious and complex song. Belonging to the family ***Muscicapidae***, its scientific name is ***Copsychus malabaricus***.

DID YOU KNOW?

White-Rumped Shamas are territorial and sing loud songs to warn others around their vicinity.

WEAVER

The Weaver is a small, vibrant bird known for its intricate nest-building skills. Weavers typically weigh around 0.7–1.7oz (20–50g). Their plumage varies widely, with males often showcasing bright yellow, red or orange feathers, while females are usually more subdued in color. Weavers primarily feed on seeds, insects and nectar. They thrive in a range of habitats, from savannas and grasslands to forests and wetlands, across Africa, Asia and parts of Europe. Their nests are often woven from grasses and leaves, forming complex hanging structures. They belong to the family ***Ploceidae*** and all the species fall under the genus ***Ploceus***.

DID YOU KNOW?

Social Weavers, a kind of Weaver birds, build large nests that can house about 100 birds.

FLAMINGO

The Flamingo is famous for its vibrant pink hue, which results from carotenoid pigments in its diet of algae, Shrimp and crustaceans. Weighing about 4.4–8.8lb (2–4kg), their height ranges from 3–5ft (0.9–1.5m) Flamingos thrive in shallow lakes, lagoons and coastal wetlands, where they use filter-feeding to obtain food. These graceful wading birds belong to the family ***Phoenicopteridae***. Their scientific name varies by the species.

DID YOU KNOW?

Flamingos are commonly found standing on 1 leg, from where we get the Flamingo yoga pose.

WHITE IBIS

The White Ibis is a wading bird with a long, curved beak that helps it catch food in shallow waters. These birds live in wetlands, swamps and coastal areas of the southeastern United States, Central America and South America. They grow about 22–27in (55.8–68.5cm) long and weigh around 2.2–2.8lb (1–1.3kg). White Ibises eat fish, insects and crustaceans. They use their strong legs to wade through water. They belong to the ***Threskiornithidae*** family and their scientific name is ***Eudocimus albus***.

DID YOU KNOW?

The oldest recorded White Ibis was at least 16 years, 4 months old when it was found in Florida in 1972.

MANDARIN DUCK

The Mandarin Duck is an exceptionally colorful bird. Male Ducks boast bright orange, green, purple and white feathers, along with a unique "sail" of feathers on their back. Whereas females have a more muted appearance with grayish-brown plumage. These ducks weigh around 15–24.7oz (430–700g). Their diet consists of seeds, plants and small aquatic animals. Native to East Asia, Mandarin Ducks are commonly found in wooded lakes and ponds. They belong to the family ***Anatidae*** and their scientific name is ***Aix galericulata***.

COMMON LOON

The Common Loon is a striking waterfowl known for its black-and-white checkered back, red eyes and sleek black head. It weighs around 6.6–13.2lb (3–6kg). A Loon feeds mainly on fish, which it catches through skilled dives in lakes and coastal waters. Often found in freshwater lakes across northern regions of Canada and USA, it migrates to coastal waters during winter, displaying remarkable adaptability. It belongs to the order ***Gaviiformes*** and the ***Gaviidae*** family. Its scientific name is ***Gavia immer***.

DID YOU KNOW?

The Common Loons can dive as deep as 200ft (60m) to catch fish!!

SPOONBILL

The Spoonbill is a large wading bird with a distinctive spoon-shaped bill. It has a primarily white body, often with a slight pinkish hue, and long, slender legs. Some species of adult Spoonbills have a crest of yellowish feathers during the breeding season. They weigh around 3.1–5.5lb (1.4–2.5kg). Spoonbills feed on small aquatic animals, such as fish and crustaceans. They inhabit wetlands, marshes and shallow lakes. They belong to the family ***Threskiornithidae*** and the ***Pelecaniformes*** order. Their scientific name differs for different species.

DID YOU KNOW?

They stretch out their legs and head when flying.

SANDHILL CRANE

The Sandhill Crane is a large, elegant bird with a predominantly gray body, accented by a striking red crown and white cheeks. It stands about 3–4ft (0.9–1.2m) tall, with a wingspan reaching up to 7ft (2m), and weighs about 6.6–11.7lb (3–5.3kg). This crane feeds on a varied diet of grains, insects, small vertebrates and aquatic plants. It inhabits wetlands, marshes and grasslands across North America. Sandhill Cranes are known for their elaborate courtship dances and migratory behavior. Belonging to the family ***Gruidae***, their scientific name is ***Grus canadensis***.

DID YOU KNOW?

The Sandhill Crane has a loud, rolling and trumpeting sound.

SWAN

The Swan is a graceful waterfowl known for its long necks and elegant appearance. They weigh around 15–33lb (6.8–15kg) and measure 4.5–5.5ft (1.3–1.6m) in length with a wingspan of 6–8ft (1.8–2.4m). Swans are primarily herbivores, feeding on aquatic plants, algae and grasses. They inhabit freshwater lakes, ponds and rivers, often nesting near the water's edge. Their striking white plumage and serene demeanor make them iconic birds worldwide. They belong to the family ***Anatidae***. The scientific name for the Mute Swan, one of the most common species, is ***Cygnus olor***.

DID YOU KNOW?

Swans can sleep while floating on the water, keeping one eye open for safety!

WHITE HERON

The White Heron, also known as the Great Egret, has sleek, white plumage, long legs and a sharp yellow bill. It can weigh up to 35oz (998g). The White Heron primarily feeds on fish, amphibians and small aquatic animals. It inhabits wetlands, marshes and coastal areas worldwide, thriving in shallow waters. It is known for its graceful flight and poised hunting stance. Belonging to the family ***Ardeidae***, their scientific name is ***Ardea alba***.

DID YOU KNOW?

They wait for the prey to come within their range and deliver a death like blow with their sharp bill.

MALLARD DUCK

The Mallard Duck is a waterfowl with a broad bill, short neck and webbed feet. It weighs up to 3lb (1.3kg). A Male Mallard is called a drake. They have a green head, while the females have dull brown heads. Their primary diet includes insects, fish and plants. They are found in the Northern Hemisphere. Their scientific name is ***Anas platyrhynchos***.

DID YOU KNOW?

Ducks do not feel cold in icy water!

TOUCAN

The Toucan is a vividly colored bird known for its large, brightly colored beak, predominantly orange with a black tip. It has a mostly black body with a white or yellow throat and chest. It can reach a length of 23.6in (60cm). A Toucan primarily feeds on fruit, insects and small animals. It inhabits tropical rainforests in Central and South America. It belongs to the family ***Ramphastidae*** and its scientific name is ***Ramphastos toco***.

DID YOU KNOW?

Even though their beaks look heavy, they are actually super light and strong.

RAINBOW LORIKEET

The Rainbow Lorikeet is a brightly colored parrot with a red bill known for its stunning blend of blue, green, orange and yellow feathers. A Lorikeet weighs around 2.6–5.5oz (75–157g). It primarily feeds on nectar, pollen and fruits using its specialized brush-tipped tongue. Found in Australia's coastal forests, woodlands and urban areas, the Rainbow Lorikeet thrives in tropical and subtropical habitats. This bird belongs to the family ***Psittaculidae***. The scientific name for the Rainbow Lorikeet is ***Trichoglossus moluccanus***.

DID YOU KNOW?

They have a special tongue covered in tiny bristles to sip sweet nectar from flowers.

HYACINTH MACAW

The Hyacinth Macaw is a stunning bird with vibrant blue feathers, highlighted by a golden-yellow patch around the eye and on the underside of the wings. As the largest macaw species, it weighs around 2.6–3.7lb (1.2–1.7kg). This striking macaw primarily feeds on nuts and seeds, inhabiting the rainforests and palm swamps of South America. It forms its nest in hollows of trees or sometimes even in riverbank holes. It belongs to the family ***Psittacidae***. The scientific name for Hyacinth Macaw is ***Anodorhynchus hyacinthinus***.

DID YOU KNOW?

The Hyacinth Macaw is 3.3ft (1m) long, making it the largest flying parrot in the world.

SCARLET MACAW

The Scarlet Macaw is a vibrant tropical bird known for its stunning red, yellow and blue feathers. They measure about 32.6in (83cm), including their tails. Scarlet Macaws primarily feed on fruits, nuts and seeds, sometimes eating unripe fruit that contains toxins other animals avoid. They inhabit the lush rainforests of Central and South America. These large parrots are a part of the family ***Psittacidae***. Their scientific name is ***Ara macao***.

DID YOU KNOW?

They can live up to 50 years in the wild and even longer in a protected setting!

GOULDIAN FINCH

The Gouldian Finch is a brilliantly colorful tropical bird. Male Gouldian Finches display vibrant plumage with a green back, purple chest and a yellow belly. Most of them have a black face, though it can differ. Females have softer colors, making them slightly less striking. These small birds weigh around 0.4–0.5oz (11–14g). They primarily eat seeds and sometimes insects. Native to northern Australia, Gouldian Finches inhabit tropical savannas and open woodlands. Belonging to the family ***Estrildidae***, their scientific name is ***Erythrura gouldiae***.

DID YOU KNOW?

Only Male Gouldian Finches can sing.

RED-VENTED BULBUL

The Red-Vented Bulbul is a lively tropical bird with a distinct appearance, featuring a black head, dark brown body and a bright red patch under its tail. It is about 7.8in (20cm) long. It primarily feeds on fruits, nectar and insects. Known for its adaptability, it inhabits open forests, gardens and urban areas across South Asia. Thus, it thrives in warm tropical regions. This bird belongs to the family ***Pycnonotidae***. The Red-Vented Bulbul's scientific name is ***Pycnonotus cafer***.

DID YOU KNOW?

The Red-Vented Bulbul's calls can be either in the form of chirps or whistles.

WOODPECKER

The Woodpecker is a striking bird, recognized for its vibrant plumage and distinctive behavior. Most species display a combination of black, white and red feathers, with some featuring yellow or green hues. Depending on the species, they vary in length from 5.9–17.7in (15–45cm). Woodpeckers primarily feed on insects, larvae and tree sap, using their strong beaks to drill into wood. They inhabit forests, woodlands and sometimes urban areas across the world. They are known for their unique drumming sounds used for communication and feeding. Woodpeckers belong to the family ***Picidae***. Their scientific name is ***Picidae***.

DID YOU KNOW?

Their feet have 2 toes pointing forward and 2 pointing backward to grip tree trunks.

KINGFISHER

The Kingfisher is a vibrant bird with a dazzling blue and orange plumage, complemented by a sharp, long beak. They can be anywhere from 3.9–17.7in (10–45cm) long, depending on the species they weigh around 1.2–1.6oz (34–45g). Their diet consists primarily of fish, insects and small aquatic creatures. Kingfishers are typically found near freshwater bodies like rivers, lakes and ponds. They are known for their exceptional diving skills and swift hunting techniques.There are about 90 Kingfisher species distributed into three families—***Alcedinidae***, ***Cerylidae*** and ***Halcyonidae***.

DID YOU KNOW?

It uses its knife-like beak to spear and tear its food, especially fish.

HORNBILL

The Hornbill is a unique bird, known for its large, curved bill, often topped with a casque. Their plumage varies by species, but typically features a mix of black, white and vibrant yellow or orange. Hornbills range in length from 15.7–23.6in (40–60cm) depending on the species. They primarily eat fruits, insects and small animals. They inhabit tropical and subtropical forests across Africa and Asia. Belonging to the family ***Bucerotidae***, their scientific name depends on their species.

DID YOU KNOW?

The smallest of all species is the Red-Billed Dwarf Hornbill measuring about 1ft (0.3m).

BARN OWL

The Barn Owl is a remarkable nocturnal bird with a distinct heart-shaped face, which enhances its hearing by funneling sound toward its ears. Known for its silent flight, this owl weighs around 14–17.6oz (400–500g). It hunts small mammals, like Mice and Voles, relying on its exceptional night vision and acute hearing. Found across open habitats, including grasslands, farms and woodlands, the Barn Owl is well-adapted to night hunting. Except Antarctica, it is found throughout the world, from the Americas to Europe and Asia. The Barn Owl belongs to the family ***Tytonidae*** and its scientific name is ***Tyto alba***.

DID YOU KNOW?

Barn Owls swallow their food whole and later spit out the bones as "pellets!"

NIGHTJAR

The Nightjar is a nocturnal bird with mottled brown, grey and black plumage, providing excellent camouflage against the forest floor. They weigh around 1.9–3.5oz (55–100g). Nightjars primarily feed on insects, catching them in flight with their wide, bristle-fringed mouths. They inhabit open woodlands, heathlands and grasslands across Europe and Asia. They thrive in habitats where their cryptic coloration offers protection during daylight hours. They belong to the family ***Caprimulgidae***. Their scientific name is ***Caprimulgus europaeus***.

DID YOU KNOW?

Nightjars have wide mouths that help them catch insects while flying.

FROGMOUTH

The Frogmouth is a nocturnal bird with mottled brown, gray and white plumage, resembling tree bark for camouflage. They have a large, flat beak and a wide, frog-like mouth. These birds measure from 9.8–21.6in (25–55cm). Frogmouths feed on insects, small vertebrates and occasionally fruit. They inhabit dense forests, woodlands and scrublands across Australia and Southeast Asia. Frogmouths belong to the family ***Podargidae***. Their scientific name is ***Podargidae***.

DID YOU KNOW?

They sleep crouching along the length of a branch during daytime.

OSTRICH

The Ostrich is the largest bird in the world. Male Ostriches weigh about 220–350lb (100–159kg) and standing up to 9ft (2.7m) tall. Whereas females are slightly smaller. Their bodies are built for running, with long, powerful legs that allow them to reach speeds of up to 45mph (72kph). Ostriches have large eyes and long necks, aiding in spotting predators. They feed on plants, seeds and insects. Ostriches inhabit savannas, deserts and open grasslands across Africa. They are flightless but incredibly fast on the ground. Belonging to the family ***Struthionidae***, their scientific name is ***Struthio camelus***.

DID YOU KNOW?

Ostrich eggs are the biggest among birds, and 1 of their eggs weighs as much as 24 Chicken eggs!

CASSOWARY

The Cassowary is a large, flightless bird found in tropical forests of New Guinea, northern Australia and nearby islands. Weighing around 99–130lb (45–59kg) and standing up to 5ft (1.5m) tall, they have strong legs, a colorful neck and a helmet-like casque on their head. They primarily feed on fruits, insects and small animals. These birds thrive in dense rainforest habitats. Cassowaries belong to the family ***Casuariidae***. All the species fall under the genus ***Casuarius***.

EMU

The Emu is a large, flightless bird with shaggy, brown-gray feathers and long, powerful legs. They weigh about 100lb (45kg) or more and can reach a height of 4.9–6.2ft (1.5–1.9m). They primarily feed on plants, seeds and insects. Emus thrive in open woodlands, grasslands and savannas across Australia. They are known for their incredible running speed, reaching up to 30mph (48kph). Belonging to the family ***Dromaiidae***, their scientific name is ***Dromaius novaehollandiae***.

PEACOCK

The Peacock is a striking bird renowned for its vibrant plumage and majestic tail feathers, called a train of feathers, that makes up 60 percent of its body. Males are called Peacocks while females are Peahens; the common term for both is Peafowl. Males, which are larger, can weigh up to 10lb (4.5kg). Peafowls are omnivores, eating seeds, insects and small animals. They are native to the Indian subcontinent but have been introduced to various parts of the world. Peafowls inhabit open forests, grasslands and park-like areas. Their vivid blue and green feathers, adorned with eye-like patterns, are used in courtship displays. They belong to the ***Phasianidae*** family and are part of the ***Pavo*** genus. With 3 species overall, the scientific name of the highly-recognized blue or the Indian Peacock is ***Pavo cristatus***.

DID YOU KNOW?

Peacocks can make a loud "mee-ow" sound like that of a cat's meow!

VICTORIA CROWNED PIGEON

The Victoria Crowned Pigeon is an elegant bird with striking blue-grey plumage, a white-tipped crest and deep maroon eyes. It is one of the largest pigeon species, weighing around 5.3–7.7lb (2.4–3.5kg). This bird feeds primarily on fruits, seeds and small invertebrates. Native of the lowland forests of New Guinea, it thrives in dense, humid habitats. Belonging to the family ***Columbidae***, its scientific name is ***Goura victoria***.

DID YOU KNOW?

This Pigeon can grow up to 29in (73.6cm) long, making it one of the largest Pigeons in the world.

GOLDEN PHEASANT

The Golden Pheasant is a brilliantly colored bird with vibrant golden-yellow and red plumage, especially striking in males with their orange-gold crest. They weigh about 22.2–24.7oz (630–700g). These birds primarily eat seeds, grains, insects and berries. They are found in forests of mountain regions of central China. They belong to the family ***Phasianidae***. Their scientific name is ***Chrysolophus pictus***.

DID YOU KNOW?

They're super speedy on the ground and often run instead of flying!

TURKEY

The Turkey is a large bird with a distinctive body color, featuring iridescent feathers that shimmer in shades of bronze, gold, green and copper. Males, called Toms, often display a fan-shaped tail and a bright red wattle on their necks. Turkeys can weigh from 11–24lb (5–11kg) and reach a size of 3.3–3.9ft (1–1.2m). They primarily feed on seeds, insects and berries. Turkeys thrive in woodlands and grasslands. They are well-adapted to a variety of forested habitats. Belonging to the family ***Meleagrididae***, their scientific name is ***Meleagris gallopavo***.

DID YOU KNOW?

A Turkey's head can change color when it's excited or scared.

GOOSE

The Goose, typically gray, white or black, is known for its strong, bulky body and long neck. Weighing around 5.5–14.3lb (2.5–6.5kg), they measure about 23.6–43.3in (60–110cm). Their diet consists of grass, grains and aquatic plants. They are often found in wetlands, lakes and grasslands across the Northern Hemisphere. They thrive in temperate and cold climates. They can survive for 30 years in a protected setting. Geese belong to the family ***Anatidae***. The scientific name for most of their species falls under the genera ***Anser*** and ***Branta***.

DID YOU KNOW?

Geese fly in a V-shaped formation to save energy!

CHICKEN

The Chicken is a widely domesticated farm bird known for its importance in egg and meat production. Male Chickens are called Roosters or Cocks and the females are called Hen. It has a plump, sturdy body with smooth feathers that can range from white, brown, black to patterned shades. Weighing about 3.3–6.6lb (1.5–3kg), they primarily feed on grains, insects and greens. Originally from jungle habitats, they are now raised worldwide on farms. Their scientific name is ***Gallus gallus***.

DID YOU KNOW?

A Hen can talk to her chicks while they are still in the egg, and the chicks can respond!

SOUTHERN GIANT PETREL

The Southern Giant Petrel is a robust seabird with a predominantly dark brown body and a distinctive pale greenish bill. It weighs around 7.7–12lb (3.5–5.5kg). It has a wingspan of about 6.5ft (2m). It primarily feeds on Squid, fish and carrion. Found around the Antarctic and sub-Antarctic islands, it thrives in cold, open ocean habitats. This bird belongs to the family ***Procellariidae*** and its scientific name is ***Macronectes giganteus***.

DID YOU KNOW?

The bird is often referred to as "stinker" by the sailors for its bad odor.

ALBATROSS

The Albatross is a majestic seabird with a wingspan that can exceed 9.8ft (3m). Their plumage is predominantly white with dark brown or black wing tips. They weigh around 5.5–14.3lb (2.5–6.5kg). Albatrosses primarily feed on Squid, fish and Krill. They inhabit the Southern Hemisphere and the North Pacific, nesting on remote islands. Belonging to the family ***Diomedeidae***, their scientific name is ***Macronectes giganteus***.

DID YOU KNOW?

They sleep while flying, taking short naps during their long journeys.

RED-BREASTED MERGANSER

The Red-Breasted Merganser is a sleek diving duck known for its slim body, long, thin bill with serrated edges and distinctive red eyes. A Male Merganser displays a striking green head, a rusty and spiky crest, while a female is more subdued with a reddish-brown head and gray body. It weighs around 31.7–47.6oz (900–1,350g). It primarily feeds on fish, using its specialized bill to grasp slippery prey. This bill is found in freshwater and coastal habitats across tundra regions. A Merganser belongs to the family ***Anatidae*** and its scientific name is ***Mergus serrator***.

DID YOU KNOW?

The Red-Breasted Merganser is super fast reaching speeds of 81mph (130kph).

BLUE-FOOTED BOOBY

The Blue-Footed Booby is a distinctive seabird known for its bright blue feet, which play a role in courtship displays. This bird has a streamlined body, with brown upperparts and white underparts and a long, pointed beak for catching fish. It weighs around 2.8–3.3lb (1.3–1.5kg). The Booby's diet consists mainly of fish, especially Sardines and Anchovies, which it catches by diving from great heights. Its habitat spans the coastal waters and islands of the eastern Pacific, notably the Galápagos Islands. Belonging to the family ***Sulidae***, the Blue-Footed Booby's scientific name is ***Sula nebouxii***.

DID YOU KNOW?

The last part of their name originates from "bobo," which in Spanish means stupid or silly, as they are unaware of their surroundings when in danger.

SEAGULL

The Seagull, commonly referred to as the Herring Gull, is known for its white and light gray body with black wingtips. They weigh around 24.7–53oz (700–1,500g). They primarily feed on fish, crustaceans and scraps. These birds are highly adaptable and often inhabit coastal areas and lakes. They are known for their loud calls and graceful flight along shorelines. Belonging to the family ***Laridae***, their scientific name is ***Larus argentatus***.

DID YOU KNOW?

They have special salt glands above their eyes to help them get rid of extra salt from seawater.

PUFFIN

The Puffin is a small seabird known for its black and white plumage and brightly colored beak, which turns vibrant orange during the breeding season. Weighing around 11.3–17.6oz (320–500g), they can fly at a speed of 55mph (88.5kph). Puffins primarily feed on small fish, such as herring and sand eels. They inhabit coastal cliffs and islands across the North Atlantic. Puffins are excellent swimmers, using their wings to "fly" underwater while catching prey. They belong to the family ***Alcidae*** and their scientific name is ***Fratercula arctica***.

DID YOU KNOW?

Puffins can flap their wings up to 400 times a minute when flying!

SNOWY OWL

The Snowy Owl is a striking bird, known for its brilliant white plumage, which provides excellent camouflage in its Arctic habitat. Males are almost pure white, while females and juveniles have dark spots and bars. These large owls weigh between 3.5–6.6lb (1.6–3kg), with a wingspan of about 3.9–4.9ft (1.2–1.5m). They primarily feed on small mammals like Lemmings and Voles. Snowy Owls inhabit tundra regions across the Arctic and northern North America. They thrive in open, treeless areas for hunting. Belonging to the family ***Strigidae***, their scientific name is ***Bubo scandiaca***.

DID YOU KNOW?

Snowy Owls have an excellent sense of hearing and vision.

PENGUIN

The Penguin is a flightless seabird known for its distinctive black and white coloration, which helps it blend into its ocean surroundings. They typically weigh around 3.3lb (1.5kg) (Little Penguin) to 88lb (40kg) (Emperor Penguin) and measure from 15.7in (40cm) (Little Penguin) to 44.8in (114cm) (Emperor Penguin) in height. They primarily feed on fish, Squid and Krill. Penguins inhabit the Southern Hemisphere, with species ranging from the Antarctic to temperate zones. Belonging to family ***Spheniscidae***, their scientific name depends upon the particular species.

DID YOU KNOW?

The Emperor Penguin is the largest Penguin and can be as tall as a 5-year-old child!